What Happens at an Amusement Park?

By Amy Hutchings

Reading Consultant: Susan Nations, M.Ed.,
author/literacy coach/consultant in literacy development

WEEKLY READER®
PUBLISHING

For a complete list of Where People Work titles,
please visit our web site at **www.garethstevens.com**.
For a free catalog describing Gareth Stevens Publishing's list of high-quality books,
call 1-800-542-2595 (USA) or 1-800-387-3178 (Canada). Our fax: 877-542-2596

Library of Congress Cataloging-in-Publication Data

Hutchings, Amy.
      What happens at an amusement park? / by Amy Hutchings ;
      reading consultant, Susan Nations.
          p. cm. — (Where people work)
      Includes bibliographical references and index.
      ISBN-10: 1-4339-0073-4   ISBN-13: 978-1-4339-0073-0 (lib. bdg.)
      ISBN-10: 1-4339-0137-4   ISBN-13: 978-1-4339-0137-9 (softcover)
      1. Amusement parks—Juvenile literature. I. Nations, Susan. II. Title.
  GV1851.H88   2009
  791.06'8—dc22
                                   2008036143

This edition first published in 2009 by
Weekly Reader® Books
An Imprint of Gareth Stevens Publishing
1 Reader's Digest Road
Pleasantville, NY 10570-7000 USA

Executive Managing Editor: Lisa M. Herrington
Creative Director: Lisa Donovan
Designer: Michelle Castro
Photographer: Richard Hutchings
Publisher: Keith Garton

The publisher thanks Playland Park in Rye, New York (www.ryeplayland.org), for its participation
in the development of this book.

Printed in the United States of America

1 2 3 4 5 6 7 8 9 10 09 08

Hi, Kids!

I'm Buddy, your Weekly Reader® pal. Have you ever been to an amusement park? I'm here to show and tell what happens at an amusement park. So, come on. Turn the page and join the fun!

Boldface words appear in the glossary.

Liz is having a special day with her dad. They are going to visit an **amusement park**.

They need **tickets** to go on the rides. They buy them at the ticket seller's booth.

tickets

Liz gets on a colorful horse. She will go up and down on the **merry-go-round**. A ride worker helps Liz put on a safety belt.

merry-go-round

9

Time for a sweet treat! A worker makes cotton candy for Liz. It is pink, fluffy, and very sticky!

cotton candy

Liz and her dad walk to another ride. A worker sweeps up **litter** to help keep the park clean.

Liz and her dad are ready to ride the roller coaster. A **mechanic** checks the ride to make sure it is safe. Soon, it will go up, up, up!

mechanic

People also work at the game booths. Liz and her dad play a fun game. Liz wins a big, blue teddy bear.

The fun isn't over yet! Liz and her dad get on the **Ferris wheel**. They will be able to see the whole park from way up high.

It was an exciting day at the amusement park! Liz is happy to take her bear home.

🐻 Glossary

amusement park: a place with rides and games

Ferris wheel: an amusement park ride made up of a large, spinning wheel with seats around its side

litter: trash on the ground

mechanic: a person who fixes machines

merry-go-round: a ride with painted horses and seats that spins around at an amusement park; also called a carousel

tickets: papers that show a fee has been paid

For More Information

Book
Roller Coaster. Marla Frazee. (Harcourt, 2006)

Web Sites
Amusement Park Fun
www.learner.org/interactives/parkphysics/coaster
Design your own roller coaster and put it to the safety test.

How Stuff Works: Roller Coasters
www.howstuffworks.com/roller-coaster.htm#
Watch a video to find out how a roller coaster works.

Index

About the Author

Amy Hutchings was part of the original production staff of *Sesame Street* for the first ten years of the show's history. She then went on to work with her husband, Richard, producing thousands of photographs for children's publishers. She has written several books, including *Firehouse Dog* and *Picking Apples and Pumpkins*. She lives in Rhinebeck, New York, along with many deer, squirrels, and wild turkeys.